You've got it all wrong

Poetry Collection

Ken Tomaro

Published by Prolific Pulse Press LLC
October 2025
Raleigh, North Carolina USA

Permission requests are to be directed to:

admin@prolificpulse.com

ISBN: 978-1-962374-62-0 Paperback

ISBN: 978-1-962374-63-7 ePub

Cover Art by Ken Tomaro

You've Got it All Wrong

You've Got it All Wrong

I remember the distinct aroma

I have spoken of it before,
these Polish donuts from my childhood
she only made them on a special occasion
or maybe a holiday here and there
and I cannot describe the smell
just that it was unique and aromatic
bringing a smile to my face always
a few years ago,
I walked into the coffee shop in my office building
and was immediately taken with the very same aroma
they couldn't tell me which pastry it was
because I couldn't describe it
I'm 52 now and sometimes I just get sad
knowing I'll never smell them again
...but it goes deeper than that, doesn't it?

I was robbed

not in the sense of some burly masked man
holding a gun to my head
but of life itself, the unseen entity
holding the gun saying,

"Give me everything. No, not the money or your wallet,
everything that was ever important to you.
I want your lives, your sanity, your ability to cope.
All of it, now!"

there was no time for fear or to fight back,
to run, scream for help
I just instinctively handed it over
like I was paying the cashier for a burger and fries
and then moved on
knowing in the back of my mind
we would meet again
and life, when we do meet again
I will take great joy
in the confused look on your face
having expected me
to crumble in a pile before you, broken
on death's doorstep
you've taken almost everything
but you'll just have to wait a little longer
for the rest

Playing God

some days I look down on the traffic
speeding down the highways
and pretend the cars and trucks are toys
running on an electric track
and I am in charge,
deciding how fast or slow they go
I push the little green button on the controller
and they speed up
push the red button and
they come to an abrupt stop
I decide who spins out in a fiery crash,
who lives or dies
no, I don't really do that
mostly I just stare at the cars and trucks whizzing by
pretending they are toys

Summer of '89

it was down at Edgewater Park
we walked along the break wall
it was late at night and dark
I imagine at one time
the cement blocks we walked along were perfect squares
but now, after years of Lake Erie slapping against them
made them worn down and smooth
there were little pockets along the surface
that collected the water making everything slippery
we could not see the lake in the darkness
only the small waves a few feet in front of us
we could see the lights of downtown miles in the distance
but nothing else, barely even ourselves
we stood on the break wall in the dark
talking about whatever teenagers talked about
we were young once
and lived our lives in the calm darkness of the unknown

Life is very much a horror movie

specifically, the scene where our unwitting victim
is walking down an empty, dark hallway
lights flickering, footsteps echoing off a worn tile floor
and with each step the hallway stretches out
becoming longer and longer
every step leads to nowhere
each step through *my* stark office hallway
leads to nowhere
and my head is filled with knowledge
of only something I know,
that another office hallway
in another building at another job
will lead to the same nowhere
so, I open the door to the stairwell
thinking this is the way out
but it's thirty-seven flights down
and with each step the stairwell stretches
a dizzy downward spiral
but I keep walking and walking
feeling the burning in my legs,
the nauseous feeling in my stomach,
my brain pounding against the walls of my skull
looking for a way out
looking for an open door that leads to sunlight, fresh air
have you ever gone out for a walk
and discovered 50 years later, you've never left?

A moment on the Radar

the leaves were still falling from the trees
in early November
I like to imagine I could feel what they feel
but really, couldn't gauge anything at all
one let go with what seemed abject terror
as if caught by complete surprise
one fell as if it were content letting go,
it was finally free
and another spiraled to the ground
like a bullet ridden jet fighter
it spun in
there were no survivors

If I believed in God

I would tell him
you didn't do such a hot job
if I believed in God
I would tell him
this masterpiece he created
is just a pile of mud and sticks
slapped together haphazardly
lacking form, function, and cohesion
but I might tell him in a gentler tone
no one wants to offend the sensitive artist
if I believed in God
I would ask him why he allowed turtles and alligators
the gift of hundreds of years of life
and gave us humans with our marrow filled shells
miles of veins and arteries
and a sponge cake of this thing called a brain
which is capable of seeing over
every single movement we make,
every color of the rainbow and then some,
allowing us to climb and jump and tumble
laugh and cry and roll our necks in circles,
hear the rain falling and the thunder
giving us the gift of pain and pleasure
and the uncertainty of which is which
I would ask him,
if I believed in God
why did you give us so little time?

The big God damn bang

But let's go back to where it all began, the Garden of Eden. The creation of man and woman. And I, God, am giving you this gift, the terrestrial paradise. Beauty no other human beings will ever lay their eyes upon. A beauty of which there are no words to describe. This is for you and only you. Go forth and explore, take in all the beauty and the glory. Go wherever you want, do whatever you want. Think and feel however you want. Just don't touch that fucking apple, is all I'm saying. Give me a fucking break, man. Don't invite me into your house for a party and tell me eat, drink, be merry, just don't sit on the couch in the family room. It's an antique, my grandmother's, in pristine condition...don't fucking touch it. If you can't accept all that can happen and all that might be, then don't put out the invitation. I'm not your dirty little science experiment.

Chickens

I am driving down the road and find myself, once again
dead center in a never-ending cycle of negative thoughts
replaying a scenario in my head over and over,
a scenario that hasn't even happened yet
but finds great ease in taking up unnecessary space
stop, rewind, replay
as if doing so somehow will put me at peace
I know no other way
there are places I'd rather be in than my own head
I just want to go home
to be in the comfort of my own four walls
but there are errands to run
I have to go to the store first
I have to stand in a line full of unhappy,
unapologetic people
all while nursing these unwarranted
and unwanted thoughts
and just as these thoughts are
spinning furiously like a record
I stop for a moment and look over to the side of the road
there are two chickens pecking away at a pile of leaves
this is not some farm in the country
or fenced in yard deep in suburbia
but a highly traveled main road
and there are fucking chickens
where chickens shouldn't be
playing like children in the tree lawn of a yard

I hover my foot over the brake
because who knows what a random chicken will do
when they see a 2-ton piece of steel
rolling down the road?
I laugh for a moment at the absurdity of what I've seen
this is truly absurd; I can't be the only one who thinks so
as I pull up to the store, I share this story
with my sister-in-law
who seems unimpressed
I think because that is what we do as a society,
we ignore the absurd and claim it as normal
but really because
she lives in a house in the woods of Georgia
and owns chickens and goats and hens,
cats, racoons, foxes, bigfoot
bigfoots? bigfeet?
what even is the plural of bigfoot?
why is any of this happening?
I just wanted some pie shells
where are these fucking pie shells?

The ones gone too soon

you keep the memories of loved ones alive,
but pay no attention to the ones still here
you don't remember the ones
who were there always when you called
and you called often
you remember the ones "gone too soon"
but the ones still here have been gone far too long
how will you ever see past the stars
when you can't even see the sky in front of you?

The devil

though he was being slick
when he created Twizzlers and cantaloupe,
the fruit that's barely trying

Reminiscence

I sit thinking about all the trips I've missed
as I'm dog sitting for money that I need
because I never don't need it
but there have been many in my lifetime
maybe not to Spain or the Amazon rainforest
or even just across the border to another state
but there have been many still

We all carry anger

I think you've got it all wrong
but I can see your grief from losing something
or the feeling of losing everything for that matter
it's hard to get up these days,
things are not as easy as they were
there is something out there for you though
what, I have no clue, I'm still looking myself
but it's there
under a pile of bricks
or a home that used to be yours
or somewhere in the woods in Bloomington Indiana
getting up is half the battle
it's saying *the point is...*
when you ask yourself *what's the point?*
It's in your breathing
you're still doing that, don't you see
your body cares enough to keep your breath moving
and so should you
I know you had a plan
and maybe it didn't go as planned
but life isn't a yellow brick road
or even a perfectly paved road with bright, clear signs
sometimes it's a slippery hill covered in wet rocks
do you remember the fearless persistence you had as a
child?

You've Got it All Wrong

it's still there
but your eyesight isn't what it used to be
so, you have to look a little harder,
squint with purpose
everything is harder now but doable
until it isn't anymore
you continue to do all these things
you say you can't do
without even realizing you're doing them

Make it stop

they were standing three feet from my desk
talking about their kids,
comparing all the sports they were in
all the after-school activities
which coach does his job, which one needs to retire
blocking the isle so I couldn't escape if I wanted to
the kids smiled, they seemed happy
but I wondered if they ever had a chance to really be kids
what with all the things their parents
thought they should be
no, I'm not being salty or bitter
toward youth and happiness
I had my time
I was an altar boy
I did somersaults
and caught fish in my mouth every Sunday
to cheers and applause from the church crowd
I belonged to the Boys and Girls club
and had my picture in the paper every other week
I had my time

and suddenly a muddle of thoughts,
a need to clear my head
to see where this poem was wandering
word of warning—
it's not a happy ending

You've Got it All Wrong

I went outside to smoke a cigarette
and one of the security guards from the building was there
he told me he lost his dad a couple of weeks ago
to a heart attack
it was sad
I'm not so compassionless as you think
after hearing so many poems about my hatred of people
and sometimes things make me sad
I talk to him here and there
went to a party at his house once
but we're not the best of friends
and it was sad
I'll never sugarcoat things for you
I'm not going to spin this
with even a remotely happy ending

death is five feet away from me
in the living room every night
it's in the car next to me at the stoplight
it's in the tree-covered hills of Georgia
the tree-covered hills of Portland
California, Arizona, Indiana

and these kids standing in front of me
too busy to be kids
won't remember their friends from junior high
they'll be pushed through football and baseball
and tennis, golf, lacrosse to socialize them
for a not-so-fulfilling life in corporate America
with their name printed on a clear piece of plastic

pinned to the fabric wall of their home away from home
so go ahead, push them to reach all *your* dreams
it won't matter, I'm sorry but it won't

death right now is sitting next to me on the couch
working on the jigsaw puzzle my sister gave up on
waiting patiently for their time to come

Breathworks

we are all tied by trauma
the first being,
sliding out of the birth canal
into the waiting arms of a cold life

The poetry you are used to

I will stand at the foot of
the hills before tomorrow
I will learn to understand
those things I don't understand at the foot of
the hills before tomorrow
I will find a soulmate
and live the American dream at the foot of
the hills before tomorrow
the whole package, the house, the dogs
I will find the strength
to lift the world with just one finger
at the foot of
the hills before tomorrow
I will learn to breathe
there are so many things
to muddle through today
before tomorrow comes
but when it does
I will stand at the foot of the hills
before tomorrow
screaming and letting go

What keeps you alive?

the pills on my desk at home
keep me alive
they keep things from swelling up
so I don't choke and die
they keep all those bad fats
from sticking around and clogging up the pipes
the pills on my desk at work
aren't as important
they keep things solid and moving along
they keep these old joints from being stiff
and the joints in my dresser drawer at home
help me forget about these stupid little pills

Bad genes

we never got a fair shot
at being a family
it's the kind of call
that makes you want to complain to management
but you know they're too busy pointing fingers
or hiding behind the golden door
both sides of the family blamed each other
and no one took responsibility
one side speaks so highly of the dead
while those still living go ignored
and the other side doesn't speak at all
everything is resting quietly under the rug
and here I sit, in the middle
with a bowl of popcorn watching this shit show
clinging to the phrase in my mind at the moment:
fuck all of you!

Taken away and taking its course

I would like to be ballooned away
like a spider
shooting out my little silken thread
and letting nature take its course
it's so random to be carried away by the wind
with your life in the hands of the universe

sometimes they only travel a few feet
and sometimes all the way across the ocean
all by instinct
that has to be it, I mean a spider doesn't think
oh shit, this is going to be rough, fuck fuck fuck! do they?
by instinct they know the job here is done
and it's time to move on

I would like to be ballooned away
letting nature take its course
letting go of all those fears
and landing somewhere different
but right now, I'm afraid I'm going to land
somewhere on a garbage scow
in the milky darkness of the Hudson river

I can't give you that

she asks me what I want for Christmas
"cash," I say, it's what I want, although more of a need
I have bills and I'm not 10 years old anymore
trainsets and race cars and board games
don't pay the bills
and a few days later she says,
"I know you wanted cash but is there anything…"
"cash!"
and a few more days later, under the small tabletop tree
were several small, wrapped packages
with my name on them
I hesitate before I ask her what *she* wants for Christmas
I already know the answer
and can't bear to hear it anymore
I don't want to tell her I can't give her her old life back
I can't give her a new set of legs
I can't give her a million dollars
and I am feeling so defeated
outside of a roof,
food in the refrigerator
mailing some letters for her
or baking an occasional cookie here and there
I can think of nothing to give her
that will mean anything at all

My boorish life (in the clouds)

a pompous psychiatrist on television
with a boorish accent, said once
the tiniest decision can shape your whole destiny
cliché? formulaic? yes
but when you're high
anything echoes profoundly

A stain in the carpet

you can't worry about your life right now
the wrinkles, the bills
that $300 tax bill due in a couple of weeks
there is a tremendous winter storm heading your way,
but you can't worry about that right now
right now, there is a large stain
on the carpet in your office
and it needs your attention
we can't have the three people
who bother to show up
pointing and questioning
it's not good for productivity

Rosemarie

in the winter of 1976
in a little suburb of Cleveland Ohio
the snow covered everything
and our little world
would stay white for the next couple of months
our mother sent us outside to shovel the driveway
for no other reason
than to give herself some peace for an afternoon
we didn't mind
and when the driveway was done
we spent some quality time
doing front flips into the piles of white we had created
after that we peeled off our wet snow suits,
the plastic bags covering our feet
and sat in front of the fireplace
a real fireplace with real, crackling wood
and a warmth that lasted the whole season
and if we had nothing else, we had the fireplace
many, many years later
I'm driving around on Christmas Eve
for no other reason than to thaw out the car
and run to the bank for my share of the rent and utilities
there are old Christmas carols on the radio
Bing Crosby, Rosemarie Clooney
and I am remembering, with a smile on my face
how easy it was
even in the midst of a paralyzing blizzard

Sometimes a dog's butthole

Cleveland in the winter isn't very pretty
but neither is a dog's butthole
there's beer, there's potholes, there's pierogies
we've won a few games
even a championship that one time
I've always said Indiana was home,
I was there for so long
but I've also said home is where the headstones are
and Cleveland is home to many
sometimes the sun comes out
then the grays aren't so gray
sometimes you'll find a cute dog walking an ugly human
sometimes a stranger will shoot you a smile
sometimes you're the dog's butthole
and sometimes you're right at home

A glittering shitshow of smash-faced adults

I hope in the end I'll be sittin' on a rainbow
at the moment I'm sitting in the office
listening to John Prine
pining for that good old country life
feeling all weepy and shit
he knew the deal
he knew how it was
and there I was
a 14-year-old boy
with a half-assed mustache
surrounded by a town full of smashed-faced kids
with torn white shoes
and ripped off shirt sleeves
driving down the dirt roads, nothing but cornfields
yelling at the cows
that to me is as colorful as the rainbow gets
I don't know what you'd call it today other than broken
a glittering shitshow of smashed-face adults
wearing pajama bottoms and $200 shoes

Not-so super

how can you swoop in to save the day
when you can't even fit your fat ass
into the flashy spandex suit?

Beyond the glass

it's cold and dark here the day after Christmas
the lights on the tabletop tree are blinking
and it helps a little
otherwise, same, same,
a few months of fanfare and buildup
the sun sets and the tree goes back to storage

I cleaned the apartment today,
changed the lightbulb in the refrigerator
and made stew from the leftover lamb my sister didn't eat
I'm tired, it's cold and dark here
and I am afraid of what's out there
beyond the glass of the balcony door
beyond the neighbor who yells at his wife,
and kids, and brother
I'm afraid I'll never find
what it is I don't even know I'm looking for
or maybe I'm afraid
I won't be able to change those things that need it

but so, I'm told,
we're only responsible for our own little part of the world
someone else's is just that,
someone else's

I wonder if it's cold and dark in Arizona.

Well, hello

wellness
on being well
or unwell, as is sometimes the case
sometimes it is dark,
like being stuck at the bottom of a well
and it's time for your annual wellness check
to make sure you and your doctor
remember each other's faces
and well, it's not that easy
"Well, you see, I can't afford it..."
and "Well, I got busy..."
"My brain is, well, mush today."
sometimes it's not so dim
"Well, I thought I was going to get screwed on that deal,
but it worked out in the end."
wellness is in the eye of the beholder
it's in a good cup of coffee
a good hand in poker or
laughing out loud when you haven't in a while
wellness is...
the day you finally crawl out
from the bottom of the well with a certain understanding
you'll be bruised and cold and wet and
"Well, it could happen again."
and it certainly could
you crawled out once and
      here's wishing you well and safe travels

About the Author

Never until recently did he consider writing poetry. Not when he slid from the womb. Not when he felt the first tingle of teen hormones. Not after he got married, divorced, moved to another city, lost a couple jobs, moved back. It just sort of happened. Ken Tomaro, self-proclaimed poet laureate of the Cleveland sewer system, has been writing poetry for a few short years. He's not famous, rich, recognized or read in schools across America. He *has* been published in several literary journals, done a couple podcasts, started the YouTube channel, *Screaming Down the Poetic Highway,* and that's pretty damn impressive. Ken Tomaro.com

You've Got it All Wrong

www.ingramcontent.com/pod-product-compliance
Lightning Source LLC
Chambersburg PA
CBHW020813130626
46554CB00006B/2417